Twin Connections

A SPECIAL BOND

Barbara Andrews

MELBOURNE, AUSTRALIA

Barbara Andrews C/- Intertype
Unit 45, 125 Highbury Road
BURWOOD VIC 3125
www.intertype.com.au

Book Layout ©2019 Intertype

Ordering Information:
Quantity sales. Special discounts are available on quantity purchases by corporations, associations, and others. For details, contact the "Special Sales Department" at the address above.

Twin Connection – Barbara Andrews. —1st ed.
ISBN 978-0-6485960-6-6

Contents

This book is dedicated to Rockney

My sister and I, you will recollect, were twins, and you know how subtle are the links which bind two souls which are so closely allied.

ARTHUR CONAN DOYLE

Preface

I have read so many articles on identical twins having a close bond and experiencing ESP. Never have I read about fraternal twins experiencing these unexplainable occurrences also.

I had a twin brother who lived with Downs Syndrome and was very severely handicapped both physically and mentally. Throughout our life we experienced this unbelievable phenomenon so often.

Sometimes over the years I would wonder if these powers were given to him because of his condition. All I knew for sure was that he was very special and the close bond we always had will stay with me forever.

Rockney passed away in 2005 at the age of sixty-one. I was devastated of course and within this book I go into detail of unexplainable incidences which have also occurred since.

I believe the human being has powers we don't understand and probably never will.

This is a story of a deep love

Acknowledgements

I thank my twin brother Rockney for sharing his life with me. He was such a special person in my life and it was a great privilege to have cared for him for so many years.

He will always be with me deep in my heart and I know that one day when it is my time we will be together again.

I also wish to thank my granddaughter Rebekah for proof reading my manuscript. She did a fantastic job and It means so much to me that it was done by her. Thank you Rebekah.

CHAPTER 1

The Closeness of Twins

My twin brother and I were born Barbara and Rockney Smith at Carrum in Victoria Australia on 11th of September 1943.

Back in those days there were no scans available as there are today so very often multiple births were a surprise at birth.

Soon after I entered the world the midwife surprisingly declared another baby was coming. I can only imagine my mother's surprise only being prepared for one baby. My twin brother was born fifteen minutes behind me.

Rockney was heavier than me at birth but I continued to grow faster and soon left him behind.

Comparing her two babies our mother knew something was not right with Rockney. He remained smaller, was harder to feed and his tiny body was much more limp.

In every photograph taken even from an early age I was always making sure Rocky was okay and tending to his needs.

It is obvious in each photo how natural it was.

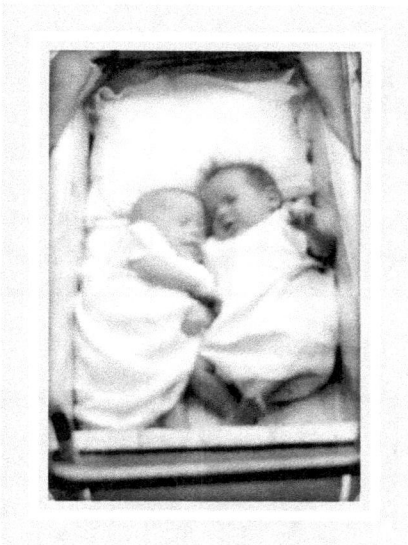

At the age of six weeks I was already growing past my twin

With our sisters Margaret and Lynette and our brother Brian

With our mother and Lynette

Rocky spent his entire life unable to speak and powerless to do anything for himself which the able bodied take for granted.

Our family moved to Cockatoo in Victoria Australia when we were seven years old. I was so thankful to be living in such a beautiful little country town.

It certainly was unique with Puffing Billy puffing its way along the narrow track through Cockatoo on its way to Gembrook.

The Cockatoo State School I attended holds many fond memories for me. Our two teachers were Mr. and Mrs. O'Leary who were more like parents to us and awarded us with a happy school life.

Whilst I attended school Rocky was home with Mum.

Whenever we went anywhere as a family, it was natural for me to carry Rocky on my back. It was no burden to me as he was very light. I still remember the feeling of content I had when he wrapped his legs around my waist and his arms around my neck. I was so blessed.

From time to time Mum would take the two of us to Melbourne to see Dr. Southby who would weigh and measure us to compare our growth. I don't understand what that ever achieved but it was always an enjoyable outing. One occasion which has stayed with me all my life was when Mum took Rocky without me and on her return home she enlightened me as to what she was told by Dr. Southby. She spoke to me alone.

"I found out today what is wrong with Rocky."

Immediately, I felt hurt inside as to me there was nothing what-so-ever 'wrong' with my twin. She continued,

"Rocky is a Mongol."

To this day I remember the deep hurt and anger I felt inside. I remember screaming at my mother "Why are you saying that, he is not" and I ran into the bush at the back of our house crying as I had never cried before. To me, as a child, the word 'Mongol' was a horrible word and how dare Mum even say it. Rocky was given a label which made him different and I failed to understand why Mum would even think that way. She was talking about my twin, my mate who was so precious to me, he was part of me.

At the dinner table Mum always sat Rocky on a chair back from the table so it was out of his reach. There was a very good reason for this,

Mum always set the table with a table cloth and every time Rocky was able to reach it he would pull the cloth and everything on the table would come crashing to the floor with an almighty bang which made him laugh uncontrollably. I always understood why he had the urge when the opportunity arose, to him he did something which made an impressive racket which amused him.

Never did I think he was being naughty. On one occasion when he had accomplished his feat our father happened to be having his lunch. Dad lacked the understanding I had and immediately became angry and attempted to hit Rocky to in his words, 'teach him a lesson'. Instinctively I jumped on top of Rocky because I knew Dad wouldn't hit me and yelled "Leave him alone, he doesn't understand."

No way would I ever allow Rocky to be hurt in any way.

Rocky could not tolerate the hot summer months and we lived so far out of town that having power connected was not an option. One summer when we were around eight, Rocky became very sick and was unable to keep any food down. Mum did the best she could but he was losing weight which he couldn't afford. She had no option but to take him to the Children's Hospital in Melbourne. As Dad drove us in I knew Rocky would be staying in hospital and the thought was heartbreaking. The nurse took him from Mum and Rocky immediately pulled her hat from her head and threw it on the floor. I smiled and thought to myself "Good on you Mate". The nurse placed him in a cot and I stayed with him while Mum spoke to the doctor. Mum explained to me

"Rocky needs to stay here for a while so the doctors can make him better."

I understood fully and I wanted Rocky to get better but when it was time to go and leave him there I felt like I was being dragged away from him forever.

In his absence, I fretted for him, I couldn't eat and I couldn't concentrate at school. People were asking me if I was okay because I was so pale. Unbeknown to me Mum enlightened Mrs. O'Leary and I recall so clearly Mrs. O'Leary sitting me on her knee and telling me

"Rocky will be home before you know it so you don't have to worry."

The day we went in to bring him home I can recall my feeling of much happiness. I was over the moon. Alas, we arrived at the hospital to witness Rocky strapped down in his cot. I began to cry and attempted to undo the straps. Mum was upset too and was told he was continually rocking in the cot and it was moving around. I told Mum he was never coming back, I felt for him so much.

I carried him out to the car and I couldn't move fast enough to get him away from there all the way telling him

"Don't worry Mate, you're going home and you'll never come here again."

Mum was never able to attend my school on Education Day when we had our schoolwork proudly on show for our parents to admire. I always understood why, as we lived so far away from the school and she never drove a car. In those days it was a rare sight to see a woman behind the wheel of a car.

However, one year as my friend's mothers were admiring their children's work I couldn't believe my eyes. As I glanced towards the door I saw my mother proudly walking into the classroom. I felt such excitement, especially when she told me

"Rocky is outside in his pusher."

I told my friends who excitedly came with me to meet him. They were making such a fuss of him and he was lapping it up. I remember standing back feeling so proud I thought my heart would burst.

When Rocky and I were ten the family moved back to our birthplace of Carrum for six months because of Dad's work.

One Sunday evening we were sitting in the lounge room when we noticed Rocky looking at the chair opposite and edging himself further and further to the edge of his chair. I could almost hear him thinking

"I can do it; I know I can."

All of a sudden he stood up and walked, for the very first time, almost ran to the chair he had been eyeing off for so long. We all praised him excitedly with disbelief. This egged him on giving him more confidence as he kept hurrying from one chair to the other laughing excitedly. From then on we encouraged him to walk on his own. His balance wasn't good so he always walked with his arms out to balance himself. He felt more secure when we held his hand. He walked very slowly but at least he was walking.

When we moved back to Cockatoo, I must say it was great to be back, he continued walking whenever he felt the urge but not very often.

On the beach at Carrum

Rocky walked for the first time at ten years

Rockney and Barbara with sister Lynette.

Back in Cockatoo and Rocky loved his new found skill

Ten years old at Cockatoo.

CHAPTER 2

The Very First Unexplainable Incident

Whilst at school one day when I was eight years old my friends and I were jumping over logs stacked in the playground at lunch time when I slipped and fell hitting my head on a log. I had stars flashing in front of my eyes for quite a while and felt very unwell for the rest of the day. I was so shy when I was a child that I kept my feelings to myself telling everyone I was okay.

By the time I arrived home I was feeling even worse and my head was aching badly. As soon as my mother saw me she asked

"Are you feeling okay Barbara?" as she placed her hand on my forehead to see if I had a temperature and feeling a huge lump. As soon as she asked me what happened I began to cry

"I fell on some logs at lunch time and hit my head.".

I'll never forget the surprised look on her face when I told her I had just finished my lunch when I fell. She immediately called to my older sister Margaret who had been home at that time having lunch with Mum and Rocky.

Rocky had been sitting on his chair back from the table happily eating his lunch when all of a sudden without warning threw himself off the chair and began rolling on the floor screaming and holding his forehead. Mum told Margaret

"Hop on your bike quickly and go and ring for the doctor."

Margaret had barely reached her bike when Mum called her back because Rocky had calmed down.

At that precise time I hit my head at school Rocky obviously felt the pain at home and reacted to it.

Mum was astounded at what she witnessed and when she told the doctor he replied" They are twins, you will most likely witness similar incidents throughout their life."

He certainly was right.

Rockney and I already had an extremely close bond and now the closeness was even more evident. Rocky was happy when I was happy and I was happy when he was happy.

We moved to Sassafras when we were thirteen and I worked on the telephone exchange as a telephonist from the age of fourteen. I remember when I received my very first salary I called into the local clothing store on the way home and bought Rocky a set of clothing. It was my first thought and I felt as though I was on cloud nine with my purchase for my mate.

After three years the family was moved to Mildura in Northern Victoria. The heat was unbearable that first summer and when I was home alone with Rocky I had a fan blowing through wet towels in front of him to keep him cool. They would dry in no time so I was continually wetting towels and replacing them.

I married in Mildura in 1963 and after some time we moved to Melbourne with our then three young children because of lack of work for Bob in Mildura. I was homesick for quite some time and I missed being close to my twin. After our fourth child was born we bought a house in Dandenong which was where our children spent their childhood.

In all those fifteen years Mum always knew whenever I was unhappy or not well because of Rocky's mood.

In those days calcium was never given during pregnancy and this affected my teeth to the extent of having to have them all extracted at the Dental Hospital in Melbourne. We decided not to tell my mother so as not to worry her. The day I had them extracted I was in the hospital overnight and my husband received a phone call from Mum asking

"What is wrong with Barbara, Rocky has spent the afternoon yelling in pain and pushing on his mouth?

Bob couldn't believe what he was hearing and replied

"She had all her teeth extracted this afternoon but we didn't want to worry you."

During all those years spent in Dandenong we always travelled to Mildura/Wentworth for a holiday twice per year. Our children adored their Uncle Rocky and were always excited to see him.

In 1973 we received the devastating news that our mother had passed away. My eldest sister Margaret who lived close to Mum and Dad cared for Rocky from the week before when Mum could no longer care for him and he seemed content with this arrangement.

Mum had often told me

"I often worry about what will happen to Rocky if anything happened to me."

I guess you never think you will ever be without your mother but I always replied

"You never have to worry about that, you should know I would always look after him."

As soon as we received the heartbreaking news we all packed a case and set off on the eight hour trip to Wentworth near Mildura.

It was late at night when we arrived and we were all so tired so we spent the night with Dad.

Early the next morning we went to Margaret's where Rocky was. Margaret met us as we got out of the car. She was very upset saying "Rocky is fretting for Mum, he won't eat his breakfast and refuses to let me do anything for him."

I hurried inside, stood at the bedroom door to witness rocky laying in bed with the sheet over his head.

"That is how he has been all morning."

I called "Rocky" and he immediately pulled the sheet down and sat up with his arms out to me. I raced to him and we hugged and cried while Margaret peeled his arms from me one at a time to wash him. She brought his breakfast in and he happily let me feed him.

We all realized that somehow he knew I was nearby and was waiting for me.

This connection made me feel proud inside but at the same time sad for Rocky's worry and concern.

After our mother's funeral, we travelled the long eight hours home to Dandenong with Rocky. Our children loved the thought of having their Uncle Rock living with us.

The sense of humour Rock had was unbelievable.

He learned to hold the cup himself to drink but I had to be there ready to take the cup from him as soon as he had finished otherwise he would throw it across the room and roar a hearty laugh as soon as it hit the floor. Whenever this had happened all I had to do was hold a cup up during the day and say

"Look Mate, what did you do?"

He would laugh that almighty laugh again. I didn't care if my actions were encouraging him, we were having fun together and that overrode everything.

In later years when grandchildren came along they delighted in passing him things so he could throw them just to hear his infectious laugh and laugh with him. I sometimes had to stop them when Rocky was unable to stop laughing because of over excitement.

CHAPTER 3

Together Again

R ocky settled in well on our return although on the first morning as I was getting him out of bed he began to cry and hugged me for quite some time. I told him I understood. This proved to me that he had an understanding of what had happened.

Our four children showed their happiness at having their Uncle Rock living with them

We didn't need words to communicate, we always had an understanding of how each of us were feeling and thinking.

I didn't have my driving licence at the time although I had been practicing some time with L plates. My mother had always told me I would never get my licence because I was too nervous and I always agreed with her. I soon realised however that I wouldn't be able to cope without driving the car now that I had Rocky living with us.

I plucked up all the courage within me and went for it. We pulled up at the police station with Rocky in the back seat but were soon told that was a 'no no' and had to leave him at home in the care of our neighbour.

I'll never forget the advice I got as my licence was passed to me. "Always remember the car can be a lethal weapon."

Everything was going along smoothly except for the colder wetter winters that Rock had not been subject to for many years. The very first winter we had him at the Dandenong hospital with bronchitis.

For Rocky's health, we decided that our sister Margaret have him in Wentworth for the winter months.

Our children played Baseball and Softball of a weekend and we usually picked up their team mates on the way. It was so comforting to see that each child we picked up wanted to sit next to Rocky.

On normal family outings, Rocky always wanted our second child Yvonne to sit next to him. We don't know what the reason was but it made her very proud of herself.

After having Rocky with us for two years I found I was pregnant with our fifth baby. Everything would have been fine except morning sickness landed me in hospital for a week. My husband had no choice but to ring Margaret to take Rocky for a while. My father brought her down that night and they took him back to Wentworth until I was back on my feet.

Donna was born five months later and Rocky came back to us three months after. Donna had Rock in her life almost from birth.

When Donna was three years old we decided to put our house on the market and move to Mildura. It seemed to be the best thing to do for many reasons. If Rocky became sick I would have my sisters nearby. Rocky's welfare had to come first.

CHAPTER 4

A Life of His Own

After three years in Mildura, I started thinking about Rock being at home with me every day. Maybe he should be given the chance to have a life of his own with his own friends. I contacted the Christie Centre in Mildura which was a day centre for the intellectually handicapped. They were very helpful and asked me to take Rock in to meet them. After this meeting they told me that yes, they could take him on a daily basis.

Panic set in as soon as I arrived home, he was to start attending the centre the next day. What had I done, I had made this decision for Rocky and there was no way of knowing if that was what he would want.

Their bus was going to call around to pick him up but no way could I let that happen, he wouldn't know what was going on so I rang Margaret, "Can you come with us on Rock's first day in the morning? He wouldn't know what was happening if I put him on the bus on his first day."

They were so nice to us at the Centre and Rock was introduced to Maureen who would be looking after him and to his hopefully new found friends. I was so pleased to hear

"You can stay with him for a while if it makes you feel better."

After quite some time we had overstayed our welcome and were reassured

"He will be well cared for. We promise."

I knew he would be but no way could I bring myself to leave him. Margaret walked to the door and called

"Come on Barbara, we have to leave."

No-one could possibly understand how I felt. I just knew I needed to stay with him, he needed me and couldn't be without me. Those were my thoughts and I was feeling very guilty at what I was doing without his permission. A big lump was welling up in my throat as I was escorted to the door. They were trying to reassure me

"We promise we will ring you if there is even a slight problem."

They just didn't understand.

I finally walked out with Margaret feeling hatred for myself for neglecting him.

I stayed by the phone all that day and it took everything within me not to get into the car and drive to the Christie Centre to be with him.

I still remember picking him up that day. He was so pleased to see me but at the same time had a very happy look on his face. My thoughts were "I think maybe this was the right thing to do."

From that day on Rocky waited patiently to hear the horn of the bus. He would reach for my hand instantly with the happiest of looks. I was now convinced it was the right thing to do to give him the chance to have the pleasure of his own friends in his life and not just me.

Everything was going so well until I received a note from the Centre asking me to give permission for Rock to go with them on a houseboat trip on the Murray River for a week. Panic set in once more, Rocky would not understand why he was away from me for so long, he would think I had abandoned him, no, he can't go. I ignored the note until I received a phone call from the Centre asking

"Why haven't you sent the note back with your permission for Rocky to go on the houseboat trip with us?".

It was only when they invited Bob and I to visit them on the second night that I even considered changing my mind.

At this time I had secured a job working with handicapped children at the local primary school. I was very content with my situation now,

Rock had a life he enjoyed with his own friends and I absolutely enjoyed my work. The school was very understanding of my situation and fully accepted the fact I may have to leave at any time if Rocky needed me.

On the day Rocky had to leave on his cruise on the Murray, I felt so uneasy. What was I doing to my mate.

I went to school as usual but my mind was not on my work and the teacher noticed. Knowing the situation she said

"You go Barbara and see your brother off."

I have never driven so fast in all my life but in spite of my efforts, I was too late as the boat had already sailed. I was told I could probably catch up with it at the Loch. Off I sped, breaking the speed limit again but this time I was in luck. The houseboat was sitting in the loch waiting for the gates to open so they could continue their journey.

I ran across the park as fast as I could to witness Rocky sitting on the deck with Maureen standing beside him holding his hand. When she saw me she pointed to me telling Rocky to look but he didn't understand even when some of his friends told him the same thing.

Maureen called out

"He'll be right, he's very happy" just as the gates opened and the boat slowly drifted away from me.

I stood there watching the houseboat with Rocky aboard very slowly drifting further and further away from me until it rounded a bend in the distance and was out of sight. I had never sobbed so much in all my life, the most special person in my life was being taken from me but I knew I had to control myself before I arrived back at work.

The teacher was so understanding and pretended she didn't notice.

I was so anxious as the second night finally arrived.

I couldn't wait to get there, my anxiety was so high but on arrival, I saw Rock before he saw me and I was so thankful I did. He was sitting on the bank in a chair with the happiest look on his face excitedly watching his friends collecting sticks to light a fire. They were interacting with him the whole time. I got tough, telling myself to stay in control so as not to ruin this moment.

We were welcomed by everyone and enjoyed being around the fire with these special people who were now part of Rock's world when the Mozzies began buzzing around and we all retreated inside.

I sat with Rocky behind the table on a bench seat holding his hand and I didn't ever want to let go. Maureen and the other instructors were very patient with me and let us stay until it was their bedtime.

I finally told Rocky

"I have to go now Mate."

As soon as those words came out of my mouth he tightened his grip on my hand and began to cry. We were ushered to the door very quickly and told

"You go, we are confident he will be okay as soon as you are out of sight."

Once again I had that tugging feeling of separation which was so hard to cope with.

I felt so good when the houseboat trip was over and I finally realised I had done the right thing to sign the permission form. He had enjoyed a great experience with his own friends for the very first time.

Rocky now had what he deserved, a life of his own with his very own friends.

He soon got to know his daily routine. I would shower him, give him his breakfast then sit him in his favourite spot in the lounge room to wait for the bus to pick him up to take him the Christie Centre. As soon as he heard the bus horn he would put his hand out to me to help him with the happiest look on his face.

One morning however it was totally different. He was sitting waiting for the bus but he was so agitated and was actually looking angrily at me making a very disapproving noise. Something had to be wrong but I had followed my routine and had his bag packed beside him and no, the bus wasn't late. I knew I must have forgotten something but for the life of me I could think of nothing.

As soon as he heard the bus he almost pushed me out the door showing his annoyance with me in no uncertain terms.

I was puzzled until I walked back inside to a completely quiet house.

That was it! I had forgotten to put the radio on playing music in the background which I did every day. I felt such guilt I wanted to get in the car and catch up with the bus to tell Rocky

"I'm so sorry Mate I understood now."

Never ever did I forget that radio again. This showed me he had a mind of his own and knew what he wanted. He, in his own way had showed his disapproval of me and I was the one not understanding. He was a good teacher.

Our grandchildren loved being with their Uncle Rock and he delighted in their attention. He was very gentle with the little ones.

I am so proud of having three sets of twin grandchildren from three of my children. Ashley and Chris. Rebekah and Sarah, Max and Billy

CHAPTER 5

A Miracle Had Transpired

Everything was going along well for Rocky and I was so happy for him.

His friends meant so much to him and just as I thought he had everything possible for the happiest life, a miracle had occurred.

Maureen sent me the most beautiful photo of Rocky and one of his friends, Maria.

It brought me to tears instantly. Rocky had the happiest most contented look on his face with his arm around Maria who was smiling the nicest smile. It couldn't have been more obvious they both had someone special in their life.

Maureen explained this scene had become a daily occurrence. Now I was absolutely convinced he was experiencing the best life possible.

Maria could communicate slightly and Rocky was unable to speak at all but that didn't matter to them. They knew how they felt and it was beautiful to see.

Why?

Tell me, what is normal?
Who is to say?
Everyone is normal
In their own special way.

Everyone is equal,
Our feelings are the same
Perhaps we cannot let you know
Tell me, who's to blame?

It isn't fair, we did no wrong
Why must we live this way
Are we being punished?
Perhaps we'll know one day.

I cannot bathe or dress myself
I cannot walk alone
I cannot make my own decisions
But I have a loving home.

This was written by my twin sister
Who knows what my thoughts would be
If only I had the privilege
Of being intellectually free.

In 1993, my children got together and organized a surprise party for the two of us for our 50th birthday. They were working on it for a whole week. They did a great job, on arrival we were escorted onto a huge stage in front of a yard full of my friends from school and Rock's friends from the Christie Centre. It was such an enjoyable surprise for the both of us and I'll never forget it.

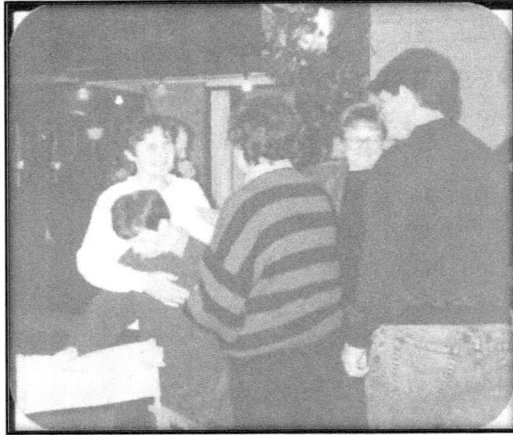

We were escorted into the back yard to be surprised by all our friends

Rocky with one of his friends from the centre.

Rockney

Fifty years have passed by Rock
And I just want to say
How very much you mean to me
On this our special day.

We have a special bond Rock
That no-one else can share
No words need be spoken
We know how much we care.

You have your private life now
Quite apart from me
You're happy with your many friends
Just how it should be.

Mum would have felt so proud today
With the little things you've learned to do
To see you happy with your life
Her dream for you come true.

I wish you a happy birthday Mate
And I really can't begin
To say how much I love you
I'm so proud that you're my twin.

Rocky always seemed to have had bad teeth but Mum always said she couldn't put him through all the pain of having them extracted.

After living with us for some years they seemed to be hurting him so I asked the doctor if he thought Rocky would cope with having them extracted. He conferred with other doctors and a dentist and they finally decided it wouldn't be a risk so an appointment was made to have it done in the hospital.

The day arrived too quickly for me but Margaret came with me to take him to the hospital. He had no idea why he was there so he wasn't one bit worried. They finally came to take him to theatre; I could feel panic welling up inside. He was on the trolley sitting up quite happily. They wheeled him away from us down the long corridor and once again I had that feeling of him being dragged away from me, that feeling that is impossible to explain.

He was half asleep when they brought him back and we were told he would cope well. We were also told, as a matter of interest, that all his teeth were baby teeth. I thought that very interesting.

Never will I forget an incident which occurred one evening.

Bob always went out on Saturday evening and Rocky and I were home alone. Rocky was sitting in his favourite spot on the lounge and I was across from him knitting. I became aware of him looking at me constantly. Before too long he slid onto the floor and in his usual way of getting around, sitting up and sliding on his bottom, made his way over to me with the biggest grin on his face and climbed up onto the lounge chair with me. There was no room for my knitting anymore but I couldn't have cared less. I hugged him happily, delighted at the contented joyful look on his face, it was one of the most blissful and wonderful moments of my life.

He had his way of letting me know how much I meant to him and I will always be thankful to him.

He was soon back at the Christie Centre and I was back at work when one day I was informed by the school Principle he had a phone call from the centre telling him they needed me right away as Rocky had fallen off a chair and appeared to be hurt. I raced there in record time to see Rocky sitting on a chair obviously in shock and as white as a sheet.

I knew instantly he was in severe pain so I immediately picked him up and carried him to the car and rang the doctor.

"I know Rocky has broken his leg or his hip, he fell off a chair at the Christie Centre and he is in a lot of pain."

He tried to assure me that wouldn't be the case but I knew I was right. On arrival at the hospital they hurried him in in a wheelchair with me in tow. I had rung my sisters who arrived just before the doctors took him for an x-ray.

The outcome was what I had expected, he had a cracked bone in his upper leg. They placed a brace on his leg and wheeled him to a private room. He seemed terrified and had no idea why he had to keep still. I will be ever thankful to my youngest son Steven who sat there for so long holding his leg in one position so it wouldn't hurt him. His patience was unbelievable.

Rock was in hospital for some time and of course I stayed with him day and night.

The hospital staff couldn't understand why I didn't go home telling me he would be well cared for. They just didn't understand why that was impossible.

Finally, Rocky was able to come home and was back with his friends at the Centre yet again but this seemed to be the turning point as things never seemed to go smoothly from then on.

CHAPTER 6

The Hardest Years Of Our Life

Rocky had gone through far too much and I was thinking maybe that is all behind us now. However, it was not to be and I was so thankful I couldn't see into the future.

Suddenly he was unable to use his bowels or bladder properly. The doctor informed me

"There is nothing wrong with him, you must try your best to encourage him and to take him to the toilet more often."

I knew the doctor was wrong but he wouldn't listen so I would have to cope.

I tried my hardest by pleading with Rock but I just knew it was to no avail as I witnessed the terrified look in his eyes. I felt so cruel but what else could I do if the medical profession refused to listen to my pleas. This went on for around six months and his discomfort and pain was getting worse.

I had had enough and someone was going to listen so I rang the doctor saying

"If you don't give me a referral to the hospital I will take him anyway and insist on him having an x-ray. He is in so much pain and I know there is something wrong."

He finally gave in to my desperate pleas and off I went to the hospital.

I didn't receive a very good reception, I was even told

"You are not only wasting our time but tax payer's money also."

I was past listening and kept insisting Rocky have an x-ray because I knew something was wrong. I was past caring what anyone thought of me. He was finally wheeled off to x-ray and I rang my sister Margaret who came to wait with me.

Finally he was wheeled back to the ward with a catheter inserted.

'One' doctor said he was so sorry because Rocky had a blocked bladder and admitted he must have been in terrible pain. I felt like saying I told you so but what good would that do now. I looked at Rocky and saw a happy relieved look that I hadn't seen for 6 months and knew he was in no more pain. That was all that mattered to me.

Rocky coped well with the catheter although he did suffer a few infections which were quickly cleared up.

Luck seemed to have run out for my mate. Even though bronchitis had been a problem throughout his life, he was now suffering more often and very often he was admitted to hospital with pneumonia.

I had given up work as Rocky needed me much more often now.

One occasion when he was very sick in hospital with pneumonia, the doctors said he may not get through it but I took no notice as I knew he would.

He was sleeping as usual when my twin grandchildren Rebekah and Sarah came for a visit with their Mum. They instantly climbed up on the bed to kiss him and Yvonne said

"No, don't do that, Uncle Rock is very sick."

I told them to go ahead, he needed a kiss so they both climbed up and kissed him. Immediately, he managed a bit of a smile and opened his eyes. It was beautiful to see.

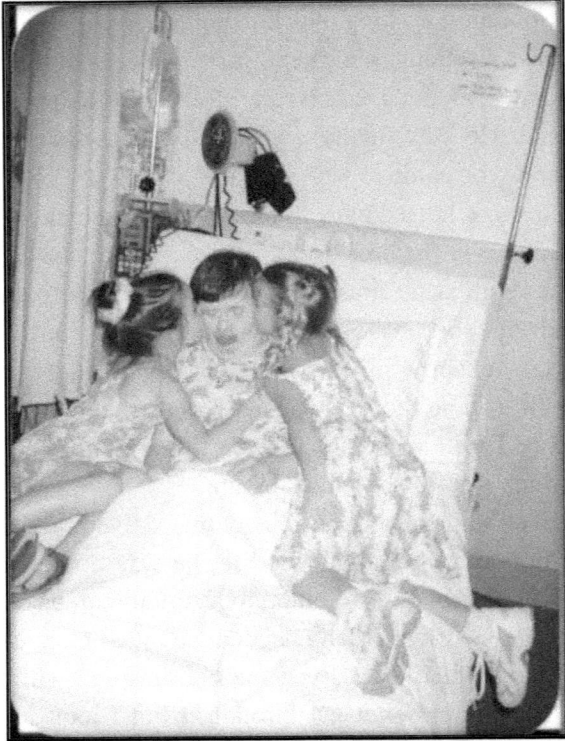

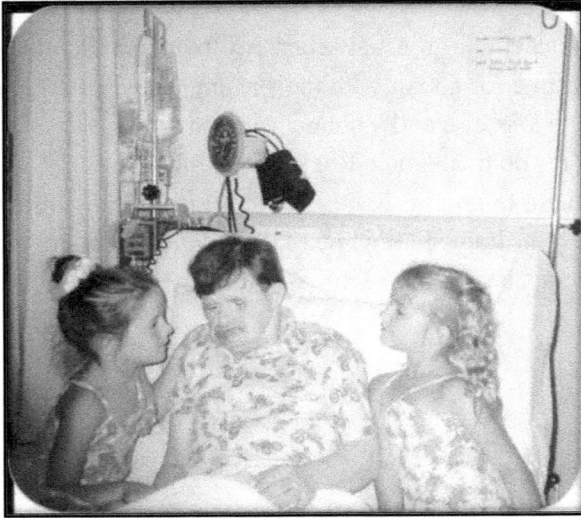

On every now frequent visit to hospital I was being told

"Do you realise you qualify for help with Rocky at home."

I always vehemently refused telling them

"I don't need help; I know Rocky and what his needs are and we are both happy with the way things are."

One morning just before it was time to get Rocky out of bed, Bob was just about to walk out the door to go to work when I heard a loud noise from Rocky's room. I raced to his bedroom door to witness the most frightening incident I've ever seen. Rocky was in a Grand Mall fit, the first one I'd ever witnessed. I called out to Bob

"Something is happening to Rocky, quick, I need help."

Bob came hurrying inside and called the ambulance.

It was devastating to see him suffering in such a way and I was so thankful Bob was still around to help. What else is Rocky going to have thrown at him?

I was told it may be a one off but the doctors leaned towards one of many. I didn't want to believe them but time proved them right.

The next fit was three weeks later. Again, it was in the early morning whilst he was in the bath. I managed to lift him out onto the floor and call my sister to help me carry him to bed. However, by the time she arrived he was already in a deep sleep.

After this incident, I was told I needed to have the bathroom remodelled so they could send someone around each morning to help me.

This made me think and I realised I did need help to get him out of bed and showered each morning for his safety so at last I accepted their offer.

There were three who came to help separately which I appreciated as Rocky got to know them and they got to know him. He was always completely relaxed with Barb and Shirley.

As soon as one of them arrived we would get him out of bed for his shower. I would have him sitting on the side of the bed and he never failed to put his arms tightly around my waist and we would hug. I thought nothing of it until one morning Barb stood back and said

"I have never seen so much love, that's beautiful."
What we thought was normal others thought extremely special.

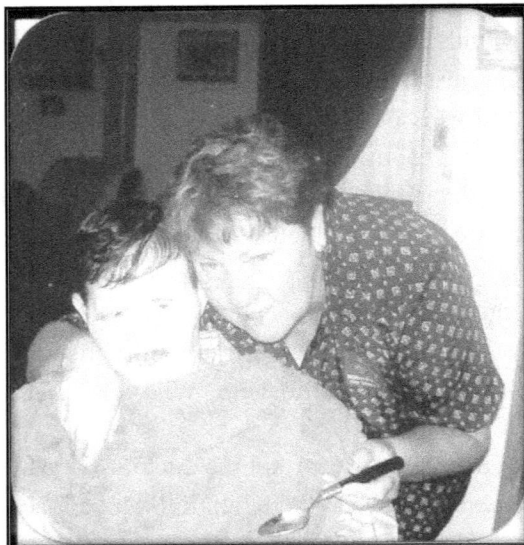

Shirley was very good with Rock, her personality helped him feel comfortable and relaxed.

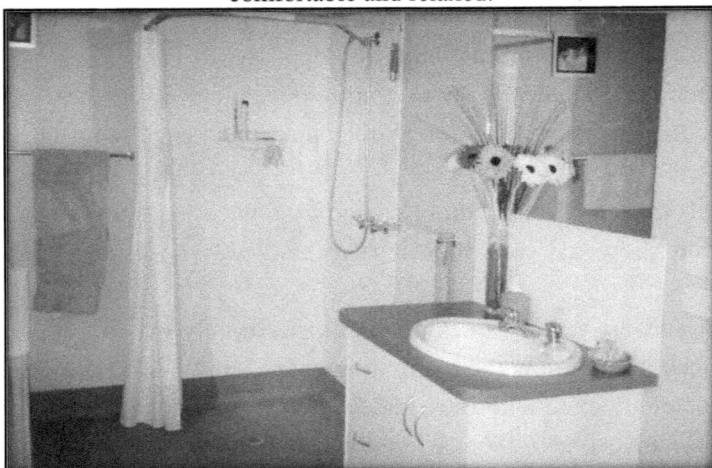

I was so thankful for the new bathroom, it was now safe and had plenty of space for the three of us.

CHAPTER 7

The Help Was Much Appreciated

Rocky continued fitting and they were becoming more frequent and weakening him significantly. In 2002 I stopped him from going to the Christie Centre so I could be with him constantly.

He stopped getting himself around on the floor and before too long had to be supported by pillows to sit up. It was heartbreaking to see him like this and I worried about him constantly.

In July and August of that year Rock succumbed to Pneumonia yet again. He was in hospital for quite some time and was becoming worse. We rang our brother Brian who came over from Tasmania.

One of Rock's lungs had collapsed and I was told by the doctors

"If you take him home he will have to go home with oxygen as we don't think his lung will re-inflate."

Both my sisters were there that night so I was told to go home and get some sleep. I was home a short time when my sister rang

"Barbara, you need to come back right away, Rocky is deteriorating and we were told he doesn't have long now."

I still remember driving back to the hospital. All the way I was thinking 'Please God help Rocky to wait till I get there."

We were told there was no hope and I could take it no longer. All of a sudden I got pain in my chest and couldn't breathe so I was rushed to emergency and put on oxygen. I didn't care what happened to me anymore.

After a while Margaret came in telling me the best news ever

"Barbara, they think Rocky has turned the corner and he's going to be okay."

His lung did inflate and soon after he was able to come home.

Brian organised a hospital bed at home for him. The Occupational Therapist also organised a commode/shower chair which made all the difference.

He was still very sick when we brought him home but he slowly improved. He is a real fighter and obviously wanted to be here. I was so thankful he got through it as I didn't think we would be having another birthday together so I wanted to do something special for him. I painted his room and got him all new bedding. I finished painting the night before our 60th birthday. That meant a lot to me.

When I saw my doctor after Rocky began to improve he wanted to be updated so I told him the story of Rocky 'turning the corner' after I was sent to emergency with severe chest pain. He replied

"You took his pain away from him."

At last someone understood and it was so comforting.

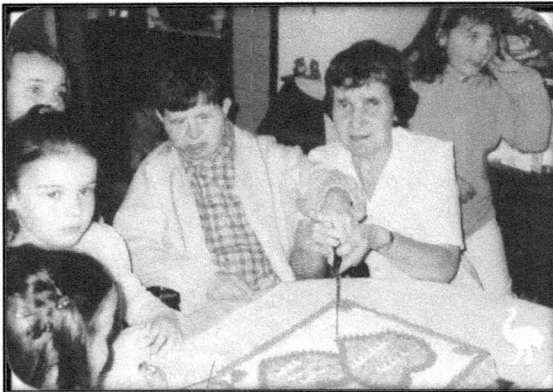

Our 60th birthday. Our last birthday party together

Thankyou Rock For Sixty Years

Sixty years Mate, I can't believe
We got this far together
It's such a great achievement
The greatest life endeavour.

Last year when you were very sick
I thought 'We won't reach fifty nine'
I underestimated your will to live
For the very first time.

When you looked into my eyes that night
I thought I'd have to let you go
That thought was so unbearable
But you fought back – how, I'll never know.

We've had to change a lot of things
We need help now, but that's okay
We've two more friends in Shirley and Barb
It's a pleasure to see them every day.

On this our sixtieth birthday Rock
I thank you for many things
For the loving look within your eyes
And the happiness you bring.

I can't express how much I love you
Our bond is stronger still
I love you Mate, with all my heart
And I always will.

Your twin sister Barbara
With you always.

I knew Rocky's health would continue to decline but I had no time to dwell on it, I lived in the now, from day to day and handled things as they came along.

He lost control of his bowels and I never knew when I would have to tend to him. I remember one evening I had to take him to the bathroom to clean him up. I had to call for Bob to stay with him while I got clean pyjamas. I went to Rock's room, put my head in the wardrobe and cried. I realised then that crying is a release of emotions and tension as I felt better when I returned to the bathroom where Rocky was waiting for me. I dressed him and before I wheeled him out I could see he was tense and uneasy so I knelt beside him, looked into his eyes and told him

"It's okay Mate, you're not a burden, you never have been and never will be, you're a good boy."

At that moment while looking into my eyes he gave me the sweetest smile. How much did he understand; it was impossible to tell? Sometimes I thought he understood more than we thought but at other times I thought no.

In 2004 we had Christmas Dinner inside so Rock could share it with us as he was becoming progressively more tired. He slept for most of the day.

Not long ago he would become so excited whenever the grandchildren walked in the room but I'm afraid that has all changed now.

He also has become progressively harder to feed; I have to spend so much time with him and feed him very slowly.

Not long into the new year it became so hard, I struggled with him for two weeks and I finally had to call his doctor as I was afraid he would become dehydrated. He was put into hospital and ended up being there for nine days on the drip. I was told there was nothing they could do as he was becoming more tired and he was not wanting to eat as his body wasn't needing it. This scared me so much but it was something I could do nothing about.

Rock's doctor wanted to have a 'peg' inserted into his stomach so he could be fed through that. I hated the idea as it scared me so much but I wondered if the solution he would be fed would make him more alert and happier. The doctors at the hospital assured me it would make no difference, that he would continue to become more tired and would end up sleeping all day every day and the solution would continue to keep him alive, maybe for years. We made a family decision on what I was told deciding to leave him alone. I was told the hospital would help me out whenever Rock needed it.

He deserved much more than this, it made me so angry.

The doctors at the hospital wanted to keep him there and 'keep him comfortable'. They told me he only had a few weeks to live.

He stopped eating altogether and was surviving on fluid going into his stomach.

For the first time in all the times he had been very sick I had to believe them. For the first time I told my mate it was okay to stop fighting. It hurt me so much but I couldn't be so selfish seeing him in this condition.

I couldn't leave him in hospital and told them I was taking him home.

For the next few weeks Palliative Care was calling in every day. I quickly learned to disconnect the fluid line each day to save them a visit then connect it again each morning.

Rock began to eat a bit each day and after a while he needed less fluid.

After a few months he was back to eating three meals a day and didn't need extra fluid. Sometimes he seemed to be back to his old self, in fact he was better than he has been for the last few years.

He stunned the doctors, they couldn't understand how this could possibly happen. They actually said they were at a loss for words.

Although he is happier, he was no stronger and slept a lot but he had happiness in his eyes. To me this is more important than anything.

I was told he wouldn't see his 59th birthday and he will be 61 in three weeks.

He definitely wants to be here and somehow he does it. He is my 'Rock'.

I didn't want to celebrate the new year of 2005 because I knew it wouldn't be a good year.

Rock's return to eating was very short lived as once again he was eating less and less. The only food I could manage to give him was a tiny bit of custard and ice-cream. He was still drinking but very little and very slowly.

I was trying my hardest to encourage him to eat until one day he kept his mouth tightly shut, smiled at me and turned his head away.

The message couldn't have been more clear. 'I know what you are doing but please leave me alone.'

It was so hard to accept his wish but I had no option.

I knew what was happening, he is now 61 years of age and that is amazing. He is becoming even weaker and I can do nothing about it.

Donna was married in February 2005 and we had to arrange for someone to sit with Rocky as he was now even too weak to sit in his wheelchair.

I will be forever grateful to the people who helped me shower Rock. Also whenever he needed equipment e.g. wheelchair, commode bathroom renovation etc. it was arranged without delay. There are a lot of nice people in this world and I sincerely thank them all.

CHAPTER 8

His Last Laugh

By March Rocky even stopped sipping water. I was beside myself and asked the Palliative Care nurse who was visiting daily if he could go on 'the drip'. Although it is purely saline I thought it may make him feel better. She rang Dr.Buckly and he agreed.

For a few weeks I learned to connect it each morning and disconnect when it finished. At least it was something.

I was so worried about him not getting his epilepsy medication but I was told there was nothing they could do.

He was now becoming so thin and I was noticing a big difference every day. I would look at him propped up with pillows and felt so frustrated and helpless. It hurt so much, I was losing my mate.

Palliative care was so supportive; I would have been lost without them. They are very special people

One day I was working on my computer where we could see each other when I heard a giggle. Rocky was looking directly at me and the giggle turned to one of his hearty laughs which I hadn't heard for so long. I was so surprised and said

"Are you laughing at me?"

He had the biggest smile and such a happy look in his eyes.

I rushed to him and hugged and played with him till he dozed off to sleep once again. I couldn't understand how he found the strength to hug me as tight as he did. They were moments I treasure to this day.

Sadly that was the last time he laughed. It proved to me how happy he was to be where he was and to have me with him. It meant the world to me.

A few days later, after being on 'the drip' for a couple of weeks he began to cough and the gurgle in his chest was terrible to hear. He was quite distressed so I immediately rang Palliative Care in a panic

"Take the drip off him, you are going against nature, his body is breaking down and is unable to cope with the fluid."

I didn't want to hear it but I knew she was right. I had all sorts of thoughts running through my head.

The next day I kept looking at him. I needed to help him and I wasn't doing that and it was driving me mad. I picked up the phone and Rang Dr' Buckley

"We can't live without food can we?"

"No, of course we can't."

"Dr. Buckley, I'm killing Rocky because I'm not feeding him."

"I'll call in to see you after this patient."

I was heartbroken and crying uncontrollably.

Before Dr. Buckley arrived, Rock became very agitated and I couldn't calm him. He suddenly went into an epileptic seizure. A short time later he had another one and he wasn't coming out of it properly. In between seizures he looked directly at me and I could do nothing to help him.

Palliative Care came around and I agreed he would have to go to hospital to have the seizures stopped. Of course, I went with him and my sisters came up later.

He was in emergency at first, half sitting up in the bed when he began making a strange noise. He was looking up into one spot in the far corner of the room and was quite agitated when I leant over in front of him to calm him. He became angry with me and pushed me away holding his arms up to the spot in the corner. I stepped back and watched him.

I have no doubt he was seeing Mum who came to reassure him. I had no doubt from that moment that this time he was leaving me.

We were informed he would have to be admitted for about 2 nights so they could get the medication right to stop the fits. Each night we were told he might not make it through the night. My sisters and I slept in the room with him. They attached a pump to him giving him morphine and another medication to calm him as he needed it. Our brother Brian came over from Tasmania.

There was now no hope for him and I told them

"He is coming home and that's that. He would want to be home where he is loved and has proved to me many times home is where he is happy."

They finally agreed and arranged an ambulance to transport him home.

The Mysterious Visitor.

I was mysteriously helped so many times when I was at my wits end and didn't know where to turn.

Rock was sent home after my insistence and against my families wishes after his last trip to hospital with new medication.

After Rock was settled I got his new medication out to make sure I understood what they had explained to Brian and I at the hospital.

We both sat down at the table with the medication in front of us.

We understood what we were told but now, we were both totally confused and couldn't remember anything they said.

I became very upset telling Brian I didn't know what to do.

Once again, at that precise moment there was a knock on the door.

I was confronted by a very kind lady asking me

"Do you need help with the medication?"

I was stunned once again and on asking her who she was all she said was she was from the hospital.

We were only minutes home from the hospital and when we left they were confident we understood their instructions.

We welcomed her inside where she explained it all, writing it all down for us. She then left after I made sure she knew how much we appreciated her visit.

Brian and I walked inside shocked, asking each other how that could possibly be.

CHAPTER 9

Our Last Days Together

Once Rock was home, Palliative Care nurses came each day. Margaret, Brian, Lynette, Bob and I were with Rock day and night. Sharon cooked tea for us each day while Rock grew weaker as time went on.

Our younger grandchildren Nikkita, Brock, Mikkaela, Tahlia, Rebekah and Sarah wrote their thoughts of their Uncle Rock.

I was so touched at the beautiful things they said, I put them on the wall beside Rocky's bed. It really brought home how much influence he had on their lives. Rock was sleeping constantly and they came in every now and then to kiss him and hold his hand. They cried every now and then. At that young age, they had complete understanding as to what was happening. I'm sure Rock knew they were there and how much they loved him.

I kept telling him he was home. I hope he understood as it would have meant a lot to him.

On the third day, early in the morning, it was one of the few times no-one was in the room with him, we heard him cough so the four of us hurried into the room to witness something unbelievable. Had I witnessed it alone I might have kept it to myself as it is beyond any understanding of a human being.

Slowly but surely Rock was 'changing' before our eyes. He stretched his neck, shut his mouth and his whole appearance changed.

He had no Downs Syndrome features at all, his skin became smooth, his eyebrows were defined, his lips and nose were small and perfect. He appeared much younger, even his shoulders were in proportion with his perfect little face. The four of us looked at him from all angles for about 20 minutes. We each calmly made our comments and couldn't believe the transformation.

As we were looking at this miracle, his mouth slowly opened and he slowly came back to the Rocky we knew.

How this actually happened we didn't know. Later we looked at younger photos of him and could see the likeness.

Were we being shown what he will soon be like with no handicap – by Rocky – or by God?

All we knew was it wasn't imagined.

I feel so very privileged to have witnessed it and I will never forget it.

The next day my cherished Rocky went into a deep coma and we were told his internal organs had broken down, but he kept breathing.

Dr. Buckley visited each night telling us he will receive a call during the night. He told us he had no idea how his heart was still beating as he had never seen it before.

I kept whispering to Rocky over and over

"It's okay to go now Mate to be with Mum, I will be okay."

Early on the Sunday morning April 17th 2005 I thought maybe he doesn't understand what I'm saying, so I asked God

"Please help Rocky to understand that he needs to go and I will be alright."

He took his last breath half an hour later.

We were all there with him and I had my arms around him. As I gently closed his eyes I told him it was okay and I felt a great relief for him.

I was going to miss him so very much but I knew there would be no more pain and he was now once again with Mum.

I love you Rock! I'll miss you so very much but you'll always be with me deep in my heart. Thankyou for our time together.

My Brother – My Mate – My Twin.

Rockney

In life on earth you were cheated
But now, I know you're free
So I'm trying not to be selfish
And wish you back with me.

The last twelve months I knew
The time was nearing for us to part
But I'll always have you with me
Deep within my heart.

The eyes are the window to one's soul
I know that is true
'Cos every time our eyes met Mate,
The bond between us grew.

I've felt so very thankful
To have you with me all those years
Now my heart is breaking and I'm trying so hard
To hold back all the tears.

I've had many highlights in my life
But one thing I always knew
The greatest privilege bestowed on me
Was looking after you.

My life will never be the same
But you're with Mum now, I know
So I'll live with cherished memories
Till it's my time to go.

Loving you always, your twin sister Barbara.
My Brother – My Mate – My Twin.

I was startled when weeks after Rock passed our son Steven told me he had witnessed the same transformation. On asking him to recall his memory, these were his words to me.

"I most certainly remember Rocky's face losing all it's wrinkles. He looked young and so called 'normal' whatever normal may be.

It didn't frighten me, it seemed to be quite natural and I could easily imagine Rocky walking amongst other people without being stared at by rude uncaring people. I have a lot of wonderful memories growing up with Rocky and he had just added another memory that will last forever."

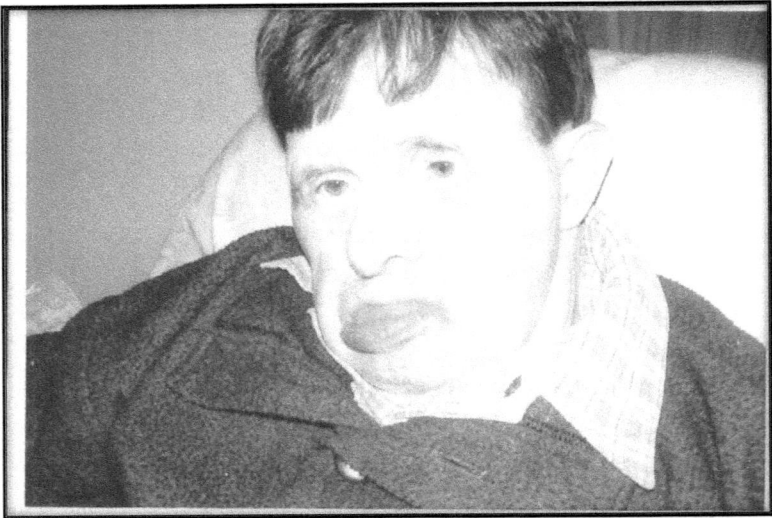

My cherished twin brother Rockney.

This was the last photo taken three weeks before he passed when he had been laughing with me for the very last time. I couldn't believe how well he looked in this photo as he was extremely weak. I will treasure it forever.

I had a copy done for each of my siblings.

CHAPTER 10

Grief is Part of a Deep Love

All of a sudden my life had changed dramatically.

After I lost my Mate, I would wake every morning to a different world, a very foreign world I had never experienced before, one I didn't like at all. I only had myself to look after. I was completely lost. I had a feeling of no purpose anymore. I felt completely alone and constantly wondered why I was here at all. I even felt guilty that I was still here and Rocky wasn't. What right did I have?

I took on ironing to keep myself as busy as I could. My garden was my hobby and because of the drought it began dying off until I had no garden at all. My feeling of 'no purpose' was as strong as ever and everywhere I went inside and out I would visualise Rocky sitting there suffering. I knew there were many happy memories but the sad ones always overrode them.

I would get up every morning to a pile of ironing. That was my life now and I didn't like it at all.

These are a few of the unexplainable incidents that happened after I lost my much loved twin.

It Wasn't a Dream.

After the heartbreaking loss of my cherished twin brother I had trouble coping with day to day living. Each night when I retired from yet another hard day to get through I would talk to Rocky, telling him

"I want to be with you Mate, it is too hard to cope on my own, I just don't feel me anymore."

For many months I had always be searching for Rock in my dreams and would awaken sadly on my own yet again.

At night, on my own, was my private time with the person I loved so dearly, who meant the world to me.

I continually felt I had lost my twin and I was desperate to find him.

One very special night I did just that, I found him.

As usual I was talking to Rocky as I drifted off to sleep.

I found myself in this extremely beautiful place where I knew I had been before, where I had sat on a garden seat in total confusion with very friendly people asking if I needed help.

This time was different; I walked along a very beautiful long pathway.

I was totally happy in this beautiful place where people were passing me by with a smile. The scenery was 'out of this world', exquisite countryside with lush green grass and inviting gardens. I was feeling secure and happy but I was on a mission which I was desperate to accomplish. I continued walking as if I knew exactly where I was going enjoying watching animals of all kinds together, happy and doing their own thing.

This was the most peaceful happy beautiful place you could ever imagine.

I finally came to a huge palatial building with extremely wide steps leading up to the biggest doors I have ever seen. Somehow I knew I was in the right place and I would soon be united with Rock. My heart was pounding with anticipation.

On entering the building, I was approached by a lady with the kindest smile I have ever seen. She asked me who I wanted then pointed to a room across the way.

As I began walking towards the room I glanced sideways to see my beloved twin Rocky, walking with a young man with dark curly hair. My heart was pounding even more as I called out to Rock.

The two of them looked at me as I ran towards them. The young man smiled and kept walking as if he knew I was there to find Rock.

As we tightly hugged each other I told Rock "I've found you at last Mate."

Rocky looked me in the eyes and did something I wasn't ready for but it was beautiful. He recited 'The Lords Prayer' word for word. He couldn't talk in this world, he never uttered a word but I didn't think this strange at all. He didn't have any disability, mentally or physically as he did here on earth but I accepted this without question.

Rock informed me

"You need to go back now."

The tears were rolling down my face as I answered

"No, you need to come with me or I will stay here with you."

I can still hear and see him looking into my eyes and telling me

"No, you must go back."

The next thing I knew was awakening to tears flooding my pillow. I was back – alone.

No-one can tell me this was a dream as even now, years later I remember every detail so vividly.

I was there with Rock and in that short time I witnessed the most beautiful place imaginable. Our world is so superficial in comparison.

It reassured my belief that one day I will be in this beautiful place and we will be together again.

Another thought I must make known is that I believe with all my heart that the young curly haired man was Max, our older brother who passed away at the age of sixteen when we were two years of age.

The people I saw in this beautiful place, now I think of it, were exactly like the people who helped me when I was at my wits end.

It has to be divine intervention; there is no other explanation for it.

It Was So Hard

After Rock went I was completely lost.

As my first birthday on my own became closer it became almost unbearable. I just didn't know how I was going to cope, I didn't want any more birthdays, it didn't seem right without Rocky. I already had thoughts that I shouldn't be here without him, it wasn't fair and it wasn't right.

The day before our birthday Bob brought the mail in. I was sitting at the table as he sorted it out placing what was obviously a birthday card on the table in front of me. He kept watching me and finally asked

"Are you going to open it?"

"I will later."

A few minutes later he went to the supermarket. At last.

As soon as Bob left I placed the envelope behind a photo on a shelf, it was never opened.

I couldn't take it any longer, I sat in Rock's chair and began sobbing uncontrollably.

I wasn't able to stop and I was worried, wondering how long Bob was going to be as he never understood whenever I showed I was upset and missing Rocky. I was beside myself and out of control.

At that precise moment the phone beside me rang.

A lady's voice with a very kind tone asked me if I was okay.

I couldn't believe it and answered

"Please tell me why you rang at this moment."

"I don't know but I suddenly began thinking of you and thought maybe you needed help."

I was stunned and managed to tell her my story. She replied

"Would you like me to come and spend the day with you tomorrow? Maybe we could walk to the river where it is nice and quiet."

She then said

"You're feeling much better now aren't you?"

I told her I was and thanked her over and over for ringing me at that specific time. I asked her who she was and she replied

"I'm from Palliative Care but I have never met you before."

If I hadn't received that phone call I don't know what would have happened. I was so thankful.

Our birthday is here again Mate
And I'm missing you so much
I long to have you with me Rock
So I can feel your loving touch.

We'll be together one day Mate
But I know you're here today
Celebrating with me
In our own special way.

I love you Rock so very much
I know you know that's true
One day in the future we'll be together
As it should be, just me and you

My First Outing

Many months after I lost my Mate I knew I had to do something about the way I felt. I was still here and I had no choice but to go on living. I didn't want Rocky to worry about me, that wouldn't be fair.

For the first time I forced myself to go shopping.

I was in a state of confusion as I drove myself to my destination. Thoughts like 'what am I doing' and 'how dare I do this' were playing over and over in my mind.

It was a dull overcast day as I made my way through the carpark to the not so inviting shopping centre. I sat in the car not liking myself at all and as I opened the car door and stepped outside, the sun miraculously broke through the clouds and a feeling of warmth and contentment filled my body and mind.

This was a feeling I had forgotten existed and I liked it. Was it confirmation from Rock that I was doing the right thing? Whether it was or not, to me it was and I smiled and thanked him.

From that day on a lot of guilt filtered from my mind and I knew I had to get on with life and do the best I could with it.

This was not an easy task but with the help of compassionate people who understood, my days slowly but surely became easier to cope with. I was smiling more often and began to seek and enjoy other people's company.

The pain of heartbreak was with me still but I was 'living again'.

I am now enjoying my new and different life knowing that Rock is with me in spirit every day.

He Didn't Know Me From A Bar Of Soap

After we had moved to Warragul from Mildura to begin a new life Donna rang me one day asking

"Will you go with me to Fountain Gate to a book signing by medium Mitchell Coombes."

I told her I couldn't possibly go as my back had been extremely painful for a couple of weeks and was not getting any better. It was so bad I could hardly walk and I was having treatment at the hospital every week day.

Donna insisted promising me she would drive slowly and carefully and would ask for a wheelchair when we got there. I had a lot of faith in Mitchell Coombes so listening to Donnas determination and against my better judgement I agreed to go.

Donna wheeled me into BigW with my two 2-year-old grandson Harry sitting on my knee. The slightest bump was so painful but the worst was over, we were there.

There was a long line of people waiting for Mitchell so we quickly took our place in the line which was growing rapidly.

There were 20 or more people in front of us when Mitchell began signing books. He treated each and every one of them the same politely signing their book, thanking them for coming and wishing them a nice day.

Finally it was our turn. Donna positioned the wheelchair in front of his desk and stood beside me. What happened next we were not ready for. He stared me in the eyes smiling and I explained

"I am not normally in a wheelchair but I have hurt my back."

He smiled again and said

"I must tell you this, there is someone standing behind you."

He then looked at Donna saying

"No, it isn't your father, he is still with us isn't he?"

Before Donna could answer he looked back at me and said

"It is your brother and there is such a special bond between you. I have never seen a stronger love between two people."

Both Donna and I began to cry as Mitchell continued

"He is telling me he is with you constantly and knows how much you miss him and he wants you to be happy. He has his arms around you right now."

Over and over he told me he has never seen such love.

Donna said

"He is Mum's twin brother."

"Yes that's right." Mitchell replied with a smile.

We then thanked him and began to move away when he called

"Wait, your brother is asking me to give you a hug."

He hugged me tightly and whispered

"This is from your twin brother and he is passing you a yellow Rose."

That was the end of me staying in control. Maureen who looked after him at the Christie Centre sent me a yellow Rose when I lost Rock and I had planted a yellow Rose bush in a pot in memory of Rock and I have always taken a photo of the first bloom every season since.

We hung around for a while to see if he spoke to anyone else, but no, he signed their book and wished them a nice day as he did those before us.

It was such a special message from Rocky which I will never forget

CHAPTER 11

Messages to My Twin

A year or more has passed now Mate
I know that's true
But no-one seems to understand
The love I have for you.

I keep as busy as I can
But they don't know how I feel
Without you here I'm all alone
My life, it isn't real.

I feel as though I'm cheating you
Living my life alone
They don't understand why I'll welcome
The day God calls me home.

I'm told that I don't have the right
To think the way I do
'Cos I have a loving family
Who needs me just like you.

Way down deep inside me
I have this hurt, this pain
No-one could ever understand
And I could never explain.

Never could I explain to anyone
The feeling I have within
I long so much to hold your hand
To be with you once again.

I know there's a reason we're here on earth
Mine was very clear
But I can't see a reason anymore
Now that you're not here.

Eight Long Years

Every day I remember
The many hugs we shared
You were so weak, but still you managed
As I helped you out of bed.

I'm remembering the last time you laughed Mate
That memory is etched so deep
I rushed to you and we hugged so tight
Then you fell asleep.

It broke my heart to watch you suffer
I could never wish you back again
'Cos I know that now you're happy Mate
And you are free of pain.

I know you're always with me
As I live from day to day
I feel your love and closeness
In a very special way.

I'll love you forever Rock.
My Brother, My Mate, My Twin.

Our Special Day

I think of you every day Mate
I have so much love for you
But today I miss you even more
And I feel so lonely too.

I know you're here beside me
But what I miss so much
Is the love I always saw in your eyes
And our hugs that meant so much.

If only I could feel once more
The hugs we had each day
I miss you so much Rock, it hurts
Since the day you went away.

Our special day is here again
And I am all alone
But I know it's not forever
As someday I'll be home.

Nine Years Have Passed

I'm remembering the day you left me
The day we had to part
I understand you had to go
But Mate, it broke my heart.

I sit in your chair and remember
The sad and happy times we had
Your chair is where I feel closest to you
I try my hardest not to be sad

I feel so privileged we were together
For all those many years
I love you so much, I truly do
It's too hard to fight the tears.

On this day especially
I remember the love I saw in your eyes
The many hugs we had together
It was so hard to say goodbye.

I can't feel those hugs you gave me now
But Rock, we're not truly apart
'Cos you're with me every day Mate
Deep within my heart.

Ten Years On

I miss you every day Mate
Even though it's been ten years
I look at your photo and talk to you
And still I fight back tears.

You were my life, my everything
I treasure the years with you
I treasure the special moments we shared
The special love between us too.

The day you left I felt a gap
That no-one could possibly fill
Until this day, after all this time
That gap is with me still.

I know your suffering is over
I know you're happy and free
One day Mate, I don't know when
Once again it will be you and me.

Until that day I must go on
Living my life with us apart
With my memories and my love for you
Deep within my heart.

Eleven Long Years

Today my heart is breaking
As I think back eleven years
The day I had to say goodbye
The beginning of many tears.

No-one knows how much I miss you Mate
As the days and years go by
I feel so sad when I think of you
No matter how hard I try

I still can feel our daily hugs
And see the love within your eyes
It broke my heart but I knew the time was near
That I had to say goodbye.

It broke my heart to see you suffer
You didn't deserve what you went through
That's over now and I'm trying to focus
On the many happy times with you.

I loved your sense of humour
How you sat so close to me
We had so many special moments Mate
They're locked in my heart eternally.

I love you Rock with all my heart
My brother, my mate, my twin
We'll be together one day Mate
One day – but I don't know when.

Twelve Long Years Without My Mate

Why am I so privileged
That I can look back all those years
And still see the love within your eyes
On those special moments shared.

I'm remembering all the fun times,
The day you threw your cup and laughed all day
The day you sat too close to our birthday cake
And grabbed a chunk when I looked away.

All I said was "Rocky"
And you laughed that hearty laugh and couldn't stop
We had the same sense of humour Mate
You certainly were my Rock.

Our special moments were many
The Saturday evenings we shared a chair
When I sat beside you those last few weeks
No need to talk, we knew how much we cared.

I will always miss you so much Mate
It seems like yesterday
As I held you lovingly in my arms
As you slowly passed away.

I know you're now free of handicap
And totally free of pain
I also know when the time is right
We'll be together again.

I have you deep in my heart Rocky, always and forever.

Rocky was the best teacher I knew. He had a mind of his own which I loved. He taught me so much about caring for others. He was the most caring person I knew. His many hugs were full of love. He taught me so much about happiness by laughing at me and with me. He taught me about unconditional love, he was full of it. He taught me tolerance of other people by never making a judgement of another person in his life.

He was great company. Every time we were on our own in the evening he would keep looking at me until before long he would make his way over and climb onto my chair with me. There the two of us would sit together. The look on his face was complete happiness. Very special moments I will treasure the rest of my days.

Most of all he taught me acceptance of the inevitable which I thought could never be done. He taught me all this without ever uttering a word. A very powerful thing.

I was so privileged to have had him in my life. I cannot possibly convey how much I miss him and love him. He WAS my life, he was Rocky, my brother, my mate, my twin.

About the Author

This is my story depicting my life with my cherished twin brother Rockney, the extremely close bond we always had and many unexplainable incidences that occurred between us.

Rocky was born with Downs Syndrome and was extremely handicapped both physically and mentally.

Although he never uttered a word in his life we always understood what each other were thinking. We didn't need words.

He was a very special person in many ways who taught me much about life.

I have written our story with much love in his honour.

www.ingramcontent.com/pod-product-compliance
Lightning Source LLC
LaVergne TN
LVHW021545080426
835509LV00019B/2851